Janusz Korczak's Children

Janusz Korczak's Children

by Gloria Spielman
illustrations by Matthew Archambault

KAR-BEN
PUBLISHING

KAR-BEN PUBLISHING
A division of Lerner Publishing Group, Inc.
241 First Avenue North
Minneapolis, MN 55401 USA
1-800-4KARBEN

For reading levels and more information, look up this title at www.lernerbooks.com.

Library of Congress Cataloging-in-Publication Data

Spielman, Gloria.
    Janusz Korczak's children / by Gloria Spielman.
        p. cm.
    Includes bibliographical references.
    ISBN 978–1–58013–255–8 (lib. bdg. : alk. paper)
    ISBN 978–1–58013–638–9 (eb pdf)
    1. Korczak, Janusz, 1878–1942—Juvenile literature. 2. Educators—Poland—
Biography—Juvenile literature. 3. Jews—Poland—Biography—Juvenile literature.
4. Physicians—Poland—Biography—Juvenile literature 5. Jewish orphanages—
Poland—Warsaw—History—Juvenile literature. 6. Holocaust, Jewish (1939–1945)—
Poland—Warsaw—Juvenile literature. 7. Warsaw (Poland)—History—20th
century—Juvenile literature. I. Title.
LB775.K6272S65 2007
943.8'4—dc22
    [B]   2006011859

Manufactured in the United States of America
3 - 41657 - 7769 - 11/9/2018

For David, my mother and fwsky — G.S.

To all of my students. — M.A.

A Warsaw Childhood

From his window, Henryk Goldszmidt watched the janitor's son playing with his friends. Their games seemed to be such fun. How he wished he could play too. But Henryk's family was wealthy, and his mother wouldn't let him play in the street with the poor, ragged children.

Henryk didn't understand grown-ups. They were supposed to look after children, but so often they treated them badly. How could teachers beat their pupils? Why did adults push children aside on the tramcars?

Henryk's parents, Celia and Jozef, didn't understand him, either. Henryk spent hours playing with toys and loved his imaginary worlds, but as he grew older, his parents began to worry. Why was their teenage son still playing childish games? His mother worried that he had no ambition. His father called him a clod, an idiot, and a crybaby.

Henryk dreamed of creating a world in which no child would be unloved or poor. Perhaps it would be a world without money. Then there would be no rich or poor children—and they could all play together.

When Henryk was eleven, his father became ill. His mother had to raise money to pay his medical bills and feed their children. She sold their belongings and rented out rooms in their house. Henryk worked too. He tutored the children of rich friends.

Seven years later, Jozef died and Henryk's life became gloomier than ever. He escaped his dull, dreary days by writing poems, plays, and stories. But when an editor poked fun at his work, he stopped writing and decided to do something more useful. He would become a doctor.

Janusz Korczak–Doctor

The young medical student still
remembered the ragged street children he
had been forbidden to play with. Henryk
became a regular visitor in the poorest
Warsaw neighborhoods. He taught the
children to read and told them stories.
They eagerly awaited the kind, red-haired
young man who always had a smile or
a piece of candy for them.

Henryk began writing again. He wrote about people so poor they couldn't feed their children. He wrote of life in damp, overcrowded rooms. He wrote about the pampered lifestyles of the rich.

Newspapers and magazines published his writings. People began calling Henryk Goldszmidt by his pen name, Janusz Korczak. His stories about the poor fascinated the well-to-do. They became eager to meet Warsaw's famous doctor-writer. Some wealthy families wanted so much to meet him that they pretended their children were ill.

Everyone knew that Dr. Korczak never refused to visit the home of a sick child. Their tricks made Dr. Korczak furious, but he knew the high fees they paid allowed him to buy medicines for his poorer patients. Many doctors wouldn't treat children whose parents couldn't pay, but Dr. Korczak was different. His free medicines, nighttime house calls, and low fees angered many pharmacists and doctors. But Dr. Korczak's young patients loved him. His warm smile, playful antics, and funny stories convinced the most frightened child to drink his soup or take her medicine.

Janusz Korczak—Father of Orphans

Yet Dr. Korczak was restless. What more could he do to help all those poor children? Neither medicine nor writing had solved their problems, so when the Orphan's Aid Society asked him to become director of a new orphanage, he accepted immediately.

For two years, he worked to create a model facility. When it opened in 1912, the orphanage at 92 Krochmalna Street was magnificent.

It was one of the first Warsaw buildings to have electricity and central heating. Huge windows let in bright light and fresh air. The orphans who came to live there were from the poorest of families. Few had seen toilets that flushed, and others had never slept on clean sheets. Some had come from another orphanage where they had been starved and clothed in rags.

Dr. Korczak and his assistant Stefa Wilczynska worked day and night to make them feel safe and protected. The youngest children were given cribs with holes in the side so they could reach out and hold hands. Dr. Korczak often got up at night to administer medicine or comfort a frightened, crying child.

Dr. Korczak cut the children's hair. He taught them to tie their shoelaces and shine their shoes. He cleared the tables, swept the floor, and peeled potatoes. Visitors who came to see the famous Dr. Korczak sometimes mistook him for the janitor. The children owned little, but Dr. Korczak gave each of them a drawer with a key to protect their simple treasures—an old photograph, a dried flower, or a button. For many the orphanage was their first real home and Dr. Korczak their first real father.

Dr. Korczak called the orphanage a "children's republic." It had its own government and a children's court where young judges were in charge of deciding how to punish their peers for bad behavior. When he felt he had done something wrong, Dr. Korczak asked the court to put him on trial.

Once he appeared before the judges for taking food without permission, once for putting a child in a corner, and once for breaking the orphanage rule that no one was allowed to slide down the banisters. But usually the young judges could not bring themselves to punish their beloved doctor too severely.

Janusz Korczak–Children's Writer

After he and Stefa had put the children to bed, Dr. Korczak would climb the stairs to the desk in his little attic room at the orphanage. He wrote articles and books for grown-ups to help them understand a child's world. He wrote stories and novels for children to help them understand the adult's world. His tales of King Matt, the child king who tried to create a society with laws that were fair to both children and adults, fascinated children all over Poland.

He became one of Poland's best-loved children's writers.

Dr. Korczak believed that children needed an outlet to share their dreams, hopes, and fears. In 1926, he started a children's newspaper and paid children a salary for the articles they wrote. He encouraged the youngest children, who could not yet write, to come into the office and dictate their stories to an editor. Many grown-ups wondered why children needed their own newspaper, but within a year Dr. Korczak's *Little Review* had thousands of young readers all over Poland.

Dr. Korczak was given his own radio show. Children and their families gathered around their radio sets and listened to his warm, comforting voice. Sometimes he told fairy tales, and other times he told funny stories. But more and more, he had to explain what was happening in the outside world.

A Changing World

The world outside 92 Krochmalna Street was changing. Adolf Hitler and his Nazi Party ruled Germany and wanted to rule the rest of Europe. Nazi soldiers invaded Poland, and Nazi planes bombed Warsaw. Hitler and the Nazis hated Jews. Dr. Korczak and the children at the Krochmalna orphanage were Jewish.

The Nazis created new laws limiting the activities of the Jewish citizens. Jewish children were not allowed to play in the parks. Jewish schools were closed. The Nazis took over Jewish businesses and factories. Business owners who gave money to support the orphanage had become penniless. They told him to close the orphanage and send the children away, but Dr. Korczak refused.

In 1940, the Nazis built a wall around seventy-three streets in Warsaw and forced all the Jews to move there. They called this area the Warsaw Ghetto. Dr. Korczak's non-Jewish friends begged him not to go into the ghetto. They wanted to hide him and keep him safe. But they couldn't take the children too.

Dr. Korczak refused to leave his children, so he, Stefa, and the teachers moved with them into the ghetto. They carried the flag of King Matt into an old school building. There was little to eat in the ghetto. Dr. Korczak was hungry and tired. But every day, he walked the streets begging for food, fuel, and money for the orphans.

The ghetto was full of disease. Children were dying daily, but Dr. Korczak managed to keep his children healthy. Yet even in the ghetto, Dr. Korczak had dreams for his children. He made sure they still went to lessons. He arranged for them to attend concerts and lectures and helped them put on plays and puppet shows for others in the ghetto.

Dr. Korczak and
the Children Leave Warsaw

The Nazis announced they were going to take the Jews to work camps in the East. Rumors spread that there was really no work and that the Jews were being taken to concentration camps and killed. One August day in 1942, Nazi soldiers burst into the orphanage. They marched Dr. Korczak, Stefa, the teachers, and their 192 children ten miles (sixteen kilometers) to the train station. The children carried with them the flag of King Matt.

People said a German soldier recognized Dr. Korczak as the author of his favorite childhood book and gave him permission to leave–alone. But Dr. Korczak refused to leave without his children.

Together Dr. Korczak and the children boarded a train. They were never seen again.

Afterword

Nobody knows exactly what happened to Dr. Korczak, Stefa, and the children after they boarded the train. Their train was bound for Treblinka, one of the many extermination camps set up by the Nazis. About one million Jews were murdered there. Today there is a symbolic cemetery at Treblinka with 1,700 stones. Each stone represents a community from which victims were deported. Only one stone bears a name. It says, simply:

Janusz Korczak (Henryk Goldszmidt) and the Children

Janusz Korczak wrote about the needs and rights of children. In 1979, inspired by Dr. Korczak's life and ideas, Poland proposed an International Declaration of Children's Rights. Ten years later, on November 20, 1989, the Convention on the Rights of the Child was passed by the United Nations.

Important Dates

1878 or 1879—Henryk Goldszmidt was born. The exact date of his birth is not known, as his father forgot to register his birth.

1898—Henryk Goldszmidt uses the pen name Janusz Korczak for the first time.

1912—Dr. Korczak opens his orphanage.

1926—Dr. Korczak first publishes *The Little Review.*

1939—The Nazis invade Poland.

1940—The Warsaw Ghetto is established.

1942—Dr. Korczak and his children board the train for Treblinka.

Bibliography

Adler, David. *A Hero and the Holocaust: The Story of Janusz Korczak and His Children.* New York: Holiday House, 2002.

Cohen, Adir. *The Gate of Light: Janusz Korczak, the Educator and Writer Who Overcame the Holocaust.* Cranbury, NJ: Associated University Presses, 1944.

Korczak, Janusz. *King Matt the First.* Translated by Richard Lourie. Chapel Hill, NC: Algonquin Books, 2004.

Korczak, Janusz. *The Warsaw Ghetto Memoirs.* Washington, DC: University Press of America, 1978.

Lipton, Betty Jean. *The King of Children: The Life and Death of Janusz Korczak.* New York: St. Martin's Griffin, 1988.